Walther Ziegler

Plato
in 60 Minutes

Translated by
Alexander Reynolds

My thanks go to Rudolf Aichner for his tireless critical editing; Silke Ruthenberg for the fine graphics; Lydia Pointvogl, Eva Amberger, Christiane Hüttner, and Dr. Martin Engler for their excellent work as manuscript readers and sub-editors; Prof. Guntram Knapp, who first inspired me with enthusiasm for philosophy; and Angela Schumitz, who handled in the most professional manner, as chief editorial reader, the production of both the German and the English editions of this series of books.

My special thanks go to my translator

Dr Alexander Reynolds.

Himself a philosopher, he not only translated the original German text into English with great care and precision but also, in passages where this was required in order to ensure clear understanding, supplemented this text with certain formulations adapted specifically to the needs of English-language readers.

Unless philosophers become kings in our states [...] or those we now call kings and potentates genuinely and competently pursue philosophy [...] there can be no respite from evil [...]. [1]

Bibliographic Information held by the German National Library: The details of the original German edition of this publication are held by the German National Library as part of the German National Bibliography; detailed bibliographical data can be found online at www.dnb.de.

© 2016 Dr Walther Ziegler
1st Edition June 2016
Jacket design and graphic design for the whole book: Silke Ruthenberg, making use of illustrations by:
Raphael Bräsecke, Creactive – Studio for Advertising, Comics & Illustrations
© JackF - Fotolia.com (image-frames)
© Valerie Potapova - Fotolia.com (image-frames)
© Svetlana Gryankina - Fotolia.com (speech-balloons)

Publisher and Printing:
BoD – Books on Demand, Norderstedt
ISBN 9783741227615

Contents

Plato's Great Discovery	7
Plato's Central Idea	19
The Path to Happiness in the Analogy of the Chariot	19
'Platonic' Love	23
The Doctrine of the Ideas	31
Learning as Recollection of the Ideas	39
The Immortality of the Soul	42
The Analogy of the Sun	50
The Analogy of the Cave	55
The Ideal State	61
Of What Use is Plato's Discovery for Us Today?	75
The Ideal State – Vision or Nightmare?	75
Plato – The Thinker Who Laid the Foundations of the West	83
We Are All Prisoners – the Ascent to the Good, the True and the Beautiful	87
Ultimate Knowledge as a Spur and Source of Strength	91
Bibliographical References	97

Plato's Great Discovery

The great discovery made by Plato (428 – 348 B.C.) was as groundbreaking as it was rich in consequences. His theory of the "Ideas" has marked and formed the whole of Western culture. His name is known all over the world. But what Plato discovered was basically something very simple. He was concerned simply to find a reliable standard of truth: a final, definitive point of orientation for our lives. Again and again he posed the question: what is right and what is wrong? How can I distinguish truth from untruth?

Already in Plato's own era – i.e. some four hundred years before Christ – this was a topic hotly debated by philosophers and citizens in the market squares of Greek cities. Everybody had his own contention and accused those who didn't share it of naivety. But to the tireless contradictors of these ancient city squares such constant disagreement seemed only natural. For the philosophers who set the tone in this age – the so-called Sophists, whose best-known representative was Protagoras – maintained that "Man is the measure of all things". Thus, it was natural that five different men should have five different ideas of "truth", since each individual, having his own standard, necessarily drew his own conclusions. A single truth binding on all, argued the Sophists, was impossible in principle.

But it was just this that Plato sought: a universally valid and absolute truth. He argued, against the Sophists, that without such a truth moral decline was inevitable, since everyone would then behave as he thought and as he pleased. Plato, for his part, sought a definitive point against which every theory, thought and action could be measured. He was concerned with just one thing: what is really true, and how can one lead a "true life"?

Therefore he was the first man to pose the core question of philosophy. The word "philosophy" is formed by combining the ancient Greek words *philia* and *sophia* and thus means, literally, 'love of wisdom' or, if we take wisdom's object to be truth: 'love of truth'. Of course, the search for the ultimate truth is a huge challenge. It is no wonder, then, that Plato, in his youth, achieved no final result. But he resolved to continue posing the question until he found an answer to it. To this end, he developed his own method: the disputation, or "dialogue". Thirty-six of Plato's forty-one books are composed as such "dialogues"

– a question-and-answer form quite new in Plato's day – showing Plato's philosophical idol, Socrates, disputing with various people on philosophically relevant themes.

At the start of these dialogues all the participants have different, and even opposite, views. But each interlocutor is obliged to answer the probing questions of the philosopher Socrates until he has either justified his view or recognized it to be wrong. These brilliantly written "disputations" enabled Plato to critique the various contradictory views of his contemporaries without settling, himself, on any idea of final truth. He even honestly admits, in the early dialogues, that he does not yet know just what such a final truth may be.

It is in this spirit that Plato has his main spokesman Socrates pronounce the famous and oft-cited dictum: 'I know only that I do not know'. This dictum literally runs:

I, as I do not know anything, do not think I do either. [2]

Plato's early dialogues always have an 'open ending'. It was enough for him to show that other philosophers, especially the Sophists, fell into self-contradiction. For example, he showed the Sophist teacher of rhetoric Gorgias, in a dialogue named after this latter, claiming that rhetoric is an essentially high and noble art. But Socrates forces him here, with his questions, gradually to concede that rhetoric, being an art of persuasion, can be used as easily in the service of an unjust cause as of a just one. In the end, Gorgias has to admit that rhetoric is less an art than a mere technique – and thus something that can be used for either good or evil.

In the dialogue Laches it is courage that is addressed. Socrates is not satisfied with his interlocutors' giving, when asked about the essence of courage, mere examples of courageous men and praising their swordsmanship, stamina, fearlessness and boldness. If this were enough, then courage would be many different things, depending upon which courageous man one considered. In the end, all the participants in the dialogue have to concede to Socrates that they have, in fact, no precise standard by which to judge what courage really consists in.

It is toward such a real or essential definition that Plato has, in each of his dialogues, his protagonist

Socrates skilfully lead the conversation. Socrates, moreover, is no mere literary figure invented by Plato. He really lived. For a long time he was Plato's own most important teacher. But since Socrates taught his pupils purely orally and never wrote a book, it was easy for Plato to put into his teacher's mouth all the doctrines which he himself held to be correct. Scholars today still find it very difficult, if not impossible, to distinguish Socrates' own original ideas from those of Plato, since almost everything we know about Socrates comes from Plato's dialogues.

There is no doubt, however, that the figure of Socrates is deliberately used by Plato to get across the central positions of his own philosophy. Plato calls the method practiced by Socrates – that of drawing his interlocutors into self-contradiction until they had to admit that their original idea was false – the "dialectic", or sometimes the "maieutic" (i.e. the "midwife") method, since Socrates, with his questions, gently brings truth to birth as a midwife does a baby, insistently repeating these questions until the contradictions in his interlocutors' views are clarified and resolved and these interlocutors themselves "give birth" to truth.

In his most famous dialogue, *The Republic*, Plato describes this manner of discussion as a "dialectical procedure of exposure". He believed the dialectical method alone to be capable of clearing aside all barbarian prejudices and false assumptions, leading men to the real ground and origin of truth, and cleansing the soul of the "barbaric filth" of preconceptions:

> [...] Then [...] only the dialectical method, by removing those hypotheses, proceeds in this way to the actual first principle in order to be securely based and, when the eye of the soul is buried in a kind of barbaric filth, it quietly draws and leads it upward [...]. [3]

Only when the dialectical method has led the soul entirely "up above" can the inner eye perceive the truth. But what is this truth? How can what is true be distinguished from what is false? In his masterpiece, *The Republic*, and in the two famous dialogues the *Phaedo* and the *Symposium*, Plato gives the decisive answer: it is the Idea of the Good. In contrast to the early dialogues, Plato found in these works which

Plato's Great Discovery

he composed as a fifty-year-old philosopher a path to real truth.

We can recognize the truth, argued Plato, if we succeed in looking beyond mere appearances. Because, beyond the everyday objects and the visible world which surrounds us, there exists a second, invisible reality: a kind of higher level of being which alone reveals to us the true world. This second reality is the realm of the Ideas. Plato draws a clear distinction between the world of the deceptive and fleeting objects which we perceive, day in day out, through our physical senses and the world of the Ideas, which reveals itself only to the inner eye.

If we wish to be rational we need to direct our minds, says Plato, only to this latter world of the Ideas:

Whenever (the soul) fixes upon what truth and reality illuminate, it observes and recognizes it and appears to have intelligence. But when it settles on anything mixed up in darkness,

> growth and decay, it forms an opinion and seems weak; it changes its views this way and that, and appears to have no intelligence. [4]

For Plato, then, it is the timeless and invisible Ideas, which stand beyond and behind all appearances, that alone are true. We can test and measure our day-to-day opinions against these Ideas and that alone will stand as true which corresponds to them or at least approximates to them. There is, for example, an Idea of the Beautiful by reference to which we can judge whether any specific thing is beautiful or ugly. And there is an Idea of Justice whereby we distinguish just from unjust and an Idea of Magnitude whereby we distinguish big from small. These Ideas are, indeed, invisible but through our minds and souls, argues Plato, we can "commune" with them.

There is, as we have said, a whole series of such Ideas by reference to which we understand the world. But Plato is concerned above all with the last, greatest and highest of them: the Idea of the Good. It is from this Idea that we must take our bearings. In *The Republic* Socrates calls the Idea of the Good the "greatest study" which precedes all other Ideas. Referring back to several analogies he explains this to one of his interlocutors as follows:

[...] You have often heard that the Idea of the Good is the most important thing to learn, in relation to which 'just' and other such terms become useful and beneficial. [5]

The Idea of the Good is so important and comprehensive because it is only through this highest Idea that every other Idea, such as that of Justice, acquires its meaning and can be applied. Once we succeed, then, in perceiving the Idea of the Good and in acting in accordance with it, we are standing, as it were, upon the firm ground of truth and are able to lead a just and happy life. Since, Plato argues, happiness and wellbeing depend decisively upon the love of truth and the leading of a virtuous life:

> For a good and honourable man or woman, I say, is happy, and an unjust and wicked one is wretched. [6]

The doctrine of the Ideas forms, without doubt, the core notion of Plato's philosophy. He was so convinced of the superior power of the Ideas that he held them to be real entities. For Plato, Ideas are not just things in our heads but have a real existence. That is to say, Plato's Ideas are not just thoughts or concepts which we use to describe or judge something but have a reality of their own which is, indeed, more real than the deceptive reality of everyday things. Or, as Plato also puts it: the invisible realm of the Ideas enjoys a higher degree of being. Whoever directs his mind to the Ideas and attempts to grasp these is

> [...] A little closer to reality and [...] turned more toward real things [...]. [7]

The Ideas, then, are, in comparison to perceptible objects, the deeper and more fundamental reality. Plato scholars have thus rightly pointed out that the doctrine of the Ideas has an ontological, an epistemological and an ethical dimension. In other words, Plato answered with this doctrine three key questions essential for all mankind. Firstly, he claimed regarding ontology (the doctrine of "what is") that the Idea of the Good represents a real force in its own right which exists, and will always exist, in the universe independently of Man.

It is a kind of eternal source of energy in which we can participate if we open our minds and souls to it. Secondly, regarding epistemology, he taught that it is the Ideas alone which enable us to distinguish truth from mere opinion and error. And thirdly, Plato even answers the ethical question regarding the right way to act by saying that it is only in the Idea of the Good that we find a binding point of orientation for our ethical and moral decisions. Whoever, then, always takes his bearings from the Ideas of the Good, the True and the Beautiful will achieve purity of soul and thereby happiness.

But in what do these strange "Ideas" consist? Where do they come from? What exactly does Plato mean when he speaks of "the Good"? And above all – how can we recognize this "Good" and live our lives in accordance with it?

Plato's Central Idea

The Path to Happiness in the Analogy of the Chariot

The path to true knowledge and thus to a happy life is, for us human beings, not an easy one. The task must be tackled anew each day. It is important that, as we do this, we keep our mind in equilibrium and continue to develop. Plato explains how we are to achieve this in his famous analogy of the chariot: the mind, in its essence, is like a chariot in which there sits a charioteer attempting to rein in two winged horses at once. These two horses stand one for human will-power and the other for Eros, i.e. the force of love. But these two powerful beasts are extremely wilful and flighty:

Therefore [...] the driving is necessarily difficult and troublesome. [8]

There exists a great danger, then, that the horses – i.e. the force of love and the force of will – may tip both themselves and the chariot into the abyss, since both "horses" represent parts of the human personality which, if care is not taken, can have very negative effects. "Eros" here, for example, stands for that whole sensual, desiring part of Man which longs for constant pleasure in the form of food and drink as well as sexual satisfaction.

The second horse, the human will, is that bold constituent part of human being which aims at success, recognition, fame and self-assertion. The charioteer, finally, stands here for the third part of what makes up a human, namely: Reason, which has the difficult task of mastering these two wilful horses, Eros and the Will, and guiding them to higher things.

Thus Reason, the strict charioteer, must rein in the force of love and guide it away from the erotic charms of the body toward higher aims. This applies especially to philosophers. Therefore Socrates poses, in the Phaedo, the following rhetorical question to one of his students:

Plato's Central Idea

> Do you think a philosopher would be likely to care much about the so-called pleasures, such as eating and drinking [...] or about the pleasures of love? [9]

As is generally the case with rhetorical questions, the student's reply merely confirms Socrates's own thought:

> I think the true philosopher would despise them. [10]

The second horse likewise, the Will, must be guided away from mere self-assertion and ambition toward prudence and respect. This mastering and ennobling of the lower faculties of the soul plays, Plato says, a decisive role not only for life after death but also for a rewarding life on earth:

> If now the better elements of the mind, which lead to a well-ordered life and to philosophy, prevail, they live a life of happiness and harmony here on earth, self-controlled and orderly, holding in subjection that which causes evil in the soul and giving freedom to that which makes for virtue. [11]

The decisive thing in this analogy of the chariot is Plato's demand that the mind, or rather Reason, should always dominate and guide the body. Because both pleasure and the will are shown as guided here by Reason as "charioteer". It is, then, the task of Reason to guide the mind upward, away from its baser instincts, on the path to virtue and truth.

'Platonic' Love

Also in his famous dialogue the *Symposium* Plato points out that Man must not simply lose himself in sensual pleasures but must rather seek to "ennoble" his baser instincts. He has, indeed, Socrates say in this famous dialogue that the love-instinct is the strongest of Man's basic needs. For Eros – as the Greeks called this instinct, personifying it as their God of Love – is the most creative and vital energy-source of all. But just for this reason, Socrates continues, its generative power must be "ennobled" and applied to higher ends. Eros, claims Plato, can be guided away from and beyond merely sexual love toward a spiritual love and even an intellectual love of science.

This he depicts in the *Symposium* very clearly. Here, Socrates resists, in an exemplary manner, sexual desire when the young man Alcibiades tries to seduce him into a homosexual adventure. Although such "pederasty" was an accepted practice in the ancient world, and Alcibiades a strikingly handsome youth, Socrates refuses the offer. Instead, he gives the young man a lecture on the four ascending forms of love.

Only in its first and lowest form, he tells the astonished Alcibiades, does Eros aim at sexual union. Already in rising to its second form it becomes a source of energy also for the love of good and beautiful attitudes to life. For a good lover, Plato argues, is as a rule also interested in doing good for his loved one and automatically does good deeds in order to please her or him. Thus, love guides us toward, and trains us in, selfless, beautiful and just actions much more effectively than our parents or relatives have been able to do:

For the guiding principle we should choose for all our days, if we are minded to live a comely life, cannot be acquired by kinship [...] (nor by) anything so well as by Love. [12]

We feel more shame, therefore, when a beloved learns of us doing something bad or morally reprehensible than when our parents learn of it:

Plato's Central Idea

> Let me say, then, that a man in love, should he be detected in some shameful act or in a cowardly submission to shameful treatment at another's hands, would not feel half so much distress at anyone observing it, whether father or comrade or anyone in the world, as when his favourite did. [13]

Thus love helps us, in its second form, to perform good deeds. In its third form, Eros can even be guided to become an intellectual love of science. But this is something few succeed in doing. Most pursue the pleasure of generation directly:

> Now, those who are teeming in body betake them rather to women and are amorous on this wise: by getting children they acquire an immortality [...] which, in their imagining, they 'for all succeeding time procure'. [14]

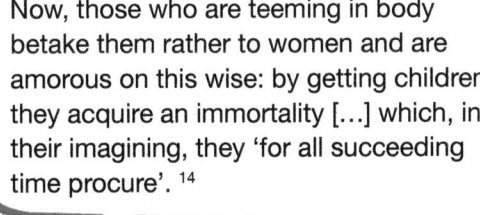

But it is not just through children that human beings can achieve a certain immortality but also through their works, i.e. by directing their power of generation toward literature or art. For, says Plato:

> [...] there are persons [...] who in their souls still more than in their bodies conceive those things which are proper for soul to conceive and bring forth. And what are those things? Prudence, and virtue in general, and of these the begetters are all the poets and those craftsmen styled 'inventors'. [15]

Inventions and scientific knowledge too, then, are products of Eros. But in its fourth and highest form love detaches itself completely from all concrete objects, even from science. Eros is now directed rather toward the Good and the Beautiful in themselves:

Plato's Central Idea

When a man has been thus far tutored in the lore of love, passing from view to view of beautiful things, suddenly he will have revealed to him, as he draws to the close of his dealings in love, a wondrous vision, Beauty in its very nature. [16]

The ascent envisaged by Plato, then, is that which starts by detaching the erotic instinct from the perception of the beloved's beautiful body and passes through the performing of beautiful and virtuous actions for this beloved's sake, then through a recognition of virtue itself as something beautiful, to end up in a lived experience of the Beautiful in itself, that is, of the pure Idea of the Beautiful:

Such is the right approach or induction to love-matters. Beginning from obvious beauties he must, for the sake of that

> highest Beauty, be forever climbing aloft, as on the rungs of a ladder, from one to two, and from two to all, beautiful bodies; from personal beauty he proceeds to beautiful observances; from observances to beautiful learning; and from learning at last to that particular study which is concerned with the Beautiful in itself and that alone; so that in the end he comes to know the very essence of beauty. [17]

It is just this that is meant by the much-cited phrase "Platonic love"; namely, to recognize and desire that which truly makes our soul happy: the Beautiful in itself. "Platonic love" is often loosely used to refer to a non-sexual, purely mental love between man and woman. But this usage is too narrow and only partly fits what Plato intended. Because Plato was concerned, above and beyond all relationships between individuals, with a spiritual love directed to the Beautiful, the True and the Good in themselves. Few of us, indeed, succeed in rising to this highest form of love. Many, Plato admits, never ascend beyond the first and lowest stage and neglect to "ennoble" the love-instinct at all. They confuse the Idea of the Good with whatever their individual desire holds to be good. Thus, Socrates explains to one interlocutor:

> But furthermore you know that to most people pleasure seems to be the Good, but to the more refined it is knowledge. [18]

Elsewhere, in the dialogue Gorgias, Plato has Socrates say, with a tinge of mockery, that the man driven solely by his instincts would vainly spend his whole life trying to fill up a barrel that had a hole in it. When his interlocutor Callicles retorts that this hole is in fact a very positive thing, since it represents the way in which hunger, and thus the pleasure of satisfying hunger, emerge and re-emerge, making all sorts of enjoyment possible, Plato's Socrates brusquely replies:

> It is a plover's life you are describing [...]. [19]

Because the plover, too, Plato has Socrates provocatively explain, spends its whole life eating, defecating and waiting to become hungry again. The "man of instinct", then, wastes his life in short-lived pleasures. But he who directs his desire to the Ideas of the Good, the True and the Beautiful experiences a much more intensive form of love:

> Generically, (love) is all that desire of good things and of being happy – Love most mighty and all-beguiling. [20]

The goal of Man, then, should consist in directing his love toward the eternal Ideas of the Beautiful and the Good. But what are these Ideas? How, for example, am I to grasp the pure Idea of the Beautiful, and on what does this Idea consist?

The Doctrine of the Ideas

First of all, one must bear in mind that the word 'idea' in ancient Greece had a somewhat different meaning from today. 'Idea' did not, at that time, bear that sense of a stroke of personal ingenuity which it bears today in such common phrases as "having a bright idea". The ancient Greek word *eidos* signified rather "form" or "archetype". Plato uses the term only in this sense. In fact, there has been, for centuries, an ongoing discussion about whether we should speak, in English, of "Plato's doctrine of Ideas" or rather of "Plato's doctrine of Forms". In any case, Plato's notion definitely was that, behind all the constantly changing things that make up everyday experience, there exist certain primal forms to which these things can be traced back as if to archetypes on which these everyday things have been modelled.

For Plato, then, the Ideas are primordial archetypes which every human being has in his head already at birth and with which he organizes and comprehends the world. Without these Ideas, argues Plato, we would simply not be able to grasp the many changes constantly going on around us and would be drowned in a chaos of random sense-impressions.

We might, therefore, provisionally take "idea" in Plato's sense to mean anything which gathers a series of individual things under a common name. Thus, we have the "idea" of a tree, which draws together all the concretely visible trees in the world under a single abstract "primordial image", namely, the concept "tree". Birch trees, fir trees, palm trees, oak trees, spruce trees and weeping willows all, indeed, differ as regards their leaves, barks and branches. But they all conform, nonetheless, to a single invisible principle of development: that archetype or recognizable "form" designated by the Greek term *eidos*. We might call it "tree-ness" or, to speak with Plato, "the Idea of the Tree". It is only thanks to this common principle or Idea that I am able to recognize the many and various growing things I encounter – be they large or small, green or withered, thick or thin – as, all of them, kinds of tree, and to immediately distinguish this kind of entity from other kinds of growing things, such as flowers or bushes.

As soon as I leave my house, then, I immediately begin to recognize, behind all the many and various sensations, smells and sounds, the original archetypes or Ideas and thus to bring order into the chaos.

There thus stand behind all those phenomena which we perceive through our senses, and the whole rich diversity of Nature, eternal Ideas of which concrete things are mere "copies". Plato emphasizes that the Idea must be there first in order for the concrete things which "commune with"this Idea to come into existence at all. The Ideas are thus the first, and the genuine, reality. This notion is very hard for us modern people to understand because we are used to starting out always from concrete things and forming only gradually, on the basis of these concrete things, certain collective concepts and abstract, overarching unities. Our modern instincts tell us that it must surely be the concrete thing that is the "original" and that the overarching concept is just a thought which we summon up later in order to conveniently classify the many concrete things. But for Plato this is not so. He insists that it is the Idea which is the more original and the more important – and he argues for this as well.

If, for example, a carpenter sets out to make a table, long before he takes up his saw and his plane he already has a precise idea of the table in his head. In order for the concrete table to come into being, the idea "table" must already exist. All the various square or round tables which such a carpenter may build throughout his long career as a craftsman merely, one might say, "commune with"this already-existent

Ideal Table.

But Plato is able to demonstrate the primacy of the Idea over the concrete object even more forcefully by the example of a geometric figure like a circle. A circle in its pure form exists nowhere in the concrete world of actually experienced Nature. It consists, by definition, of a plurality of points set all of them at precisely equal distance from a centre and not even the most carefully manufactured ceramic bowl, discus or silver coin could ever possibly satisfy this definition of points at precisely equal distance. All such concrete circular objects can be, at best, only more or less adequate "copies" of the thus-defined archetypical circle. Mathematicians and geometers, then, concern themselves never with really visible circular objects or with tracing out the shadows of these latter; their concern is rather always with the invisible Idea of "the circle *per se*", something that can only be grasped through the intellect:

> These very things they are forming and drawing, of which shadows and reflections

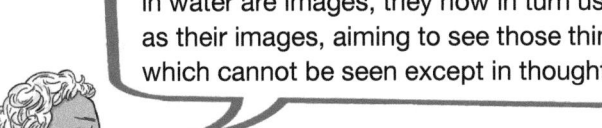

in water are images, they now in turn use as their images, aiming to see those things which cannot be seen except in thought. [21]

An equilateral triangle is another such Idea or archetype which is actually nowhere to be found in the concrete world of everyday objects. No matter how painstakingly a carpenter builds a triangular table out of three equal pieces of wood, or how carefully a geometer draws, in illustration of a theorem, such a triangular figure in the sand, what they achieve will always only be an imperfect copy of the precisely-proportioned archetype that they have in their minds. Moreover, such copies are fragile, passing things. The triangle drawn in the sand can be effaced in a moment by a gust of wind or fall of rain and even the triangle of wood will eventually rot away. But the Idea of a triangle endures forever because Ideas, being invisible, are also timeless.

This status of the Ideas as eternal, as compared to the fragile, fleeting quality of the things perceived by the senses, is, for Plato, a decisive indication that Ideas enjoy greater importance than mere phenomena and possess a higher kind of reality than these latter. All the external appearances which we grasp through our physical senses are in constant transformation and are, for just this reason, to be grasped only as fleeting "shadows". If we did not possess some prior idea of what really constitutes a human being it would be impossible to grasp at all that such apparently utterly diverse beings as a babe-in-arms, an adolescent boy, a full-grown man or woman, and a very old man really do have in common the fact of being human beings.

Let us take as a final example of the superior importance and higher reality of the invisible Ideas the specific case of the Idea of Beauty. A beautiful human being can grow old, suffer an accident, or become scarred. A beautiful vase can lose its glaze or be disfigured by a crack. But the Idea of Beauty itself, says Plato, remains unaltered by these facts. Human beings, animals, plants and other objects merely partake of, or participate in, Beauty for a short time. Then they decline and fade. The Beautiful per se, however, remains untouched by such decline, since it is incorporeal and eternal. Thus, Plato distinguishes mere beautiful things from the Idea of the Beautiful and states that:

> Though all (the multitude of beautiful things) are coming to be and perishing, it grows neither greater nor less, and is affected by nothing. [22]

Beauty, Plato explains to us here, can never be explained by any concrete shape, form or colour. Whether we find, for example, the colour red or the form of a circle beautiful or ugly will depend on the context in which this colour or this form occurs. Thus, whereas a setting sun sinking into the sea may arouse delight in us, a blood-smeared rifle-bullet may provoke rather disgust – even though the one and the other are both red and round. The beauty of a thing, then, depends neither upon a round form nor upon a red colour, nor indeed upon any other defined shape or hue, but rather solely upon whether the redness and the roundness of the thing are such as "commune with" the Idea of Beauty or not. Plato declares himself, consequently, to be bored by long, detailed explanations of why a thing is beautiful. For him the question is simple: whatever is beautiful is so insofar, and only insofar, as it participates in the Idea of Beauty:

> If anyone tells me that what makes a thing beautiful is its lovely colour, or its shape, or anything else of the sort, I let all that go, for all those things confuse me, and I hold simply and plainly […] to this: that nothing else makes it beautiful but the presence or communion (call it which you please) of absolute Beauty, however it may have been gained. About the way in which it happens I make no positive statement as yet, but I do insist that beautiful things are made beautiful by Beauty. [23]

Our sense of beauty arises, then, not from any concrete colour or shape but rather from the "communion" of certain objects with an invisible Idea.

Learning as Recollection of the Ideas

Even a child can distinguish beautiful from ugly, big from small, although it has as yet experienced little of the world. This fact that we can make such distinctions already at the very start of life is, for Plato, an indication that we must have somehow become acquainted with the Ideas of Beauty, Magnitude, and Equality, along with all the other Ideas, already before our birth. Thus, he poses the rhetorical questions:

> [...] We saw and heard and had the other senses as soon as were born, (did we not?)[...] But, we say, we must have acquired a knowledge of equality before we had these senses? [...] Then it appears that we must have acquired it before we were born. [24]

This is an important milestone in Plato's philosophy. The Ideas – such as those of Equality, Magnitude, Beauty, or Justice – do not, it appears, need to be taught to children. They are clearly already somehow present in their minds. Even a slave who has never had any contact with geometry nor even attended a school can, Plato argues, solve a whole series of geometrical problems simply by working with these fundamental Ideas which he somehow already bears within himself. In the dialogue called *Meno* Plato has Socrates demonstrate this with a young boy, who proves indeed able to answer questions regarding an equilateral rectangle without prior instruction and drawing simply on his ideas of squareness and equality. He appears to be able to work with these ideas even though no one has ever explained them to him. From this Socrates draws the following conclusion:

And if (the boy) did not acquire (these insights) in this present life, is it not obvious at once that he had them and learnt them during some other time? [25]

But when was this? Plato's answer is astonishing. It must have been before his birth. In Plato's view, not only the Ideas but also our souls existed long before we were born, so it is natural that the latter should "commune with" the former. Plato envisages human souls as actually bound together, in a kind of underworld where they sojourn before their birth, with the eternal Ideas. When a soul is then reborn into a human body, it forgets at first much of what it knew in its state of close co-existence with the Ideas. But a soul can also gradually recollect all that it saw before its rebirth, including the simple Ideas but also the Idea of Virtue:

> Seeing, then, that the soul is immortal and has been born many times and has beheld all things both in this world and in the nether realms, it has acquired knowledge of all and everything; so that it is no wonder that it should be able to recollect all that it knew before about virtue and other things [...] since, it would seem, research and learning are wholly recollection. [26]

For Plato, then, all our learning is, in reality, simply our soul's recollection of its earlier state, in which it was united with the invisible Ideas. Because the soul existed long before our birth and does not really die with our death but only leaves the body. When freed by death from the body, says Plato, the soul goes back into the realm of the Ideas.

The Immortality of the Soul

Human beings' souls are immortal. And yet, says Plato, they do not all suffer, after death, the same fate. How a person has lived is of great importance. If, already during his lifetime, he has turned his mind toward the ideas and been open, above all, to the Idea of the Good, then it is an easy matter for his soul to free itself from the body:

> But I think that if, when it departs from the body, it is defiled and impure, because it was always with the body and cared for it and loved it and was fascinated

> by it and its desires and pleasures, so that it thought nothing was true except the corporeal, which one can touch and see and drink and eat and employ in the pleasures of love [...] do you think a soul in this condition will depart pure and uncontaminated? [27]

Plato's answer here is consistent. A soul which has remained, all its life, mired in bodily needs and material stimulations will not be able, in the moment of death, to free itself completely from this body. It will wander therefore, unsaved, within the shadow realm.

Plato taught, as did Christianity some centuries later, that access to the realm of the Ideas was refused to souls who had sinned. But, whereas Christianity provided for a Purgatory in which such souls could undergo, in the afterlife, a process of purification, in Plato's philosophy there remained for those souls not yet ripe to reunite with the divine Ideas no path but that leading back into the body: i.e. reincarnation.

In the dialogue *Phaedo*, Socrates describes in great detail to his interlocutor Cebes how there are many bad souls condemned to creep, for a time, helplessly, as dark apparitions from the shadow-world, around graves and memorials, until at some point they become once again tied to a body:

> It is likely, Cebes [...] that those are not the souls of the good but those of the base, which are compelled to flit about such places as a punishment for their former evil mode of life. And they flit about until, through the desire of the corporeal which clings to them, they are again imprisoned in a body. [28]

Plato's notion of reincarnation here displays a close affinity with Hindu ideas. Some scholars have suggested that he may, on his travels, have come into contact with the Hindu doctrine of the cycle of death and rebirth. For Plato, like the Hindus, makes a person's conduct in past lives the decisive factor for the life he is reborn into. A man who has lived a low life of vice and sin is reborn as an animal of correspondingly low status:

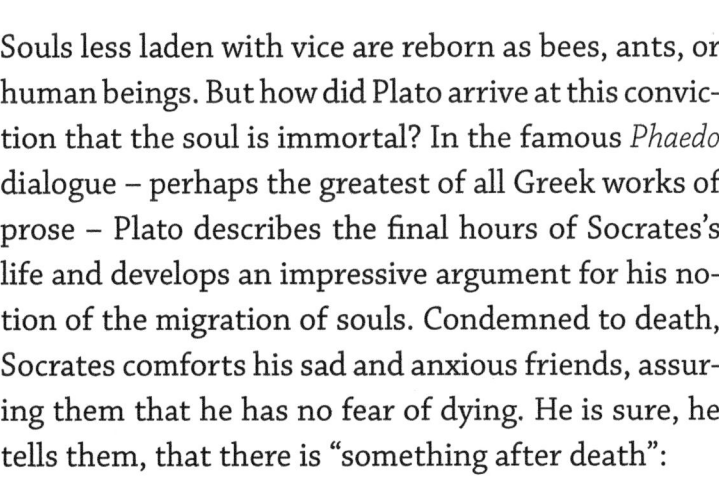

> Those who have indulged in gluttony and violence and drunkenness and have taken no pains to avoid them are likely to pass into the bodies of asses and other beasts of that sort. [...] Those who have chosen injustice and tyranny and robbery pass into the bodies of wolves and hawks and kites. [29]

Souls less laden with vice are reborn as bees, ants, or human beings. But how did Plato arrive at this conviction that the soul is immortal? In the famous *Phaedo* dialogue – perhaps the greatest of all Greek works of prose – Plato describes the final hours of Socrates's life and develops an impressive argument for his notion of the migration of souls. Condemned to death, Socrates comforts his sad and anxious friends, assuring them that he has no fear of dying. He is sure, he tells them, that there is "something after death":

> And therefore [...] I not only do not grieve but I have great hopes that there is something in store for the dead and, as has been said of old, something better for the good than for the wicked. [30]

Since the souls of the dead live on, detaching themselves from their bodies in the moment of death, a death sentence is no punishment for a true philosopher. On the contrary, the philosopher is preparing, essentially, his whole life long for such a moment. As Plato has Socrates say in these hours just before his own death, philosophizing is really nothing else than learning how to die:

> Other people are likely not to be aware that those who pursue philosophy aright study nothing but dying and being dead. [31]

Socrates is able to take death so lightly because he is convinced that death is a liberation for the soul. Because, in life, the soul really finds itself in a pitiful state:

> [...] entirely fastened and welded to the body and [...] compelled to regard realities through the body as if through prison bars. [32]

In another passage Plato even calls the body "the tomb of the soul"[33]. But the soul's immortality is, for Plato, not just a supposition. He believes it can be proven. He has Socrates propose, besides the phenomenon of the "recollection" of the Ideas, also three more proofs. For a start he points out that there are essentially just two types of things in the world: visible things and invisible ones. The visible things include, for example, chairs, tables, houses, stones, plants and animals; invisible things, on the other hand, would include such Ideas as that of the

Just, the Good, and the Beautiful. All visible things pass away: the chair can rot, the stone crumble and the house fall down. Invisible things, however, are eternal: the Idea of Justice has existed for many centuries and will continue to exist in future. Since the soul surely belongs to the class of invisible things, it follows that it must be as immortal as all the other members of this class.

Plato holds changeability to be a second proof. The body of a plant, an animal or a human being is constantly changing. First it is young and blossoms but, with time, it becomes old, fragile and susceptible to illness. But invisible Ideas such as Justice or Beauty are not subject to change. And since the soul, unlike the body, seems not to be exposed to this process of constant growth and decline, it belongs to the class of unchangeable things, which once again places it in the class of what is immortal.

Thirdly, all forms of being can be distinguished in terms of whether they move themselves or need to be moved by some other force. A stone must be rolled or thrown in order to move; it can never move by its own impulsion. It is, like everything else that requires an external source of motion, a thing that is limited and that passes away. But the case of the soul is different:

> Every soul is immortal. For that which is ever moving is immortal. [...] For every body which derives motion from without is soulless, but that which has its motion within itself has a soul. [...] But if this is true – that that which moves itself is nothing else than the soul – then the soul would necessarily be ungenerated and immortal. [34]

We have hereby arrived at the central notion of Plato's philosophy. In every human life, the immortal soul has the chance to liberate itself from the body by developing itself to higher levels. But since, in daily life, we far too frequently allow ourselves to be distracted by petty concerns and sensations, we often forget to pay attention to what is essential. Plato's entire philosophy turns, in the end, around the question of how we can come to know the eternal Ideas of the Good, the True and the Beautiful. Plato's best-known answers to this question are to be found in two famous analogies: the "analogy of the sun" and the even more renowned "analogy of the cave".

The Analogy of the Sun

In his analogy of the sun Plato describes the soul's path to knowledge in terms inspired by the process of sight. Just as our eyes need light in order to perceive objects clearly and distinctly, so too does the soul need the Idea of the Good if it is really to behold truth.

Plato begins this analogy of the sun by describing the normal act of everyday vision. Were it not for the rays of the sun, he says, objects would not be illuminated and the eye would not be able to distinguish light or dark or colour of any sort. In other words, light is the decisive factor in our perceiving anything at all through our eyes. We know the world more or less clearly depending on how adequately it is illuminated:

> When (the eyes) see clearly, I think, what the sun illuminates, sight seems to be in the very eyes themselves. [35]

Plato's Central Idea

Plato then goes on to speak of reason and the soul in terms analogous to the optical process of vision:

> Then think about the function of the soul in this way. Whenever it fixes upon what truth and reality illuminate, it observes and recognizes it and appears to have intelligence. But when it settles on anything mixed up in darkness, growth and decay, it forms an opinion and seems weak; it changes this way and that and appears to have no intelligence. [36]

The essential thing, then, is to open the soul to light, i.e. to the Idea of the Good. Because it is to the existence of the Good alone that we owe all true knowledge. The light is responsible not only for our being able to see and know things but also for these things' very existence. Because it is the light of the sun alone, argues Plato, that awakens the visible world to life. Plato has Socrates assume this to be the view of one of his interlocutors in the dialogue containing the analogy of the sun:

51

> You will agree, I think, that the sun not only gives things that can be seen the ability to be seen, but also their generation, growth and nurture, without being the generation itself. [37]

The apparently small qualification which Plato introduces with the last words of this passage – "without being the generation itself" – is in fact a distinction of great consequence. It has been taken up by the whole of Western philosophy and theology as the "ontological difference". The phrase sounds weighty and obscure but what is meant by it is really very simple. The "sun" – i.e. the Idea of the Good – generates, indeed, the light which makes possible the generative development – the existence, growth and becoming – of all beings. But "it itself isn't generation". That is to say, the Good is not itself subject to change and becoming and is thus not a being among beings. The "sun" – i.e. the Good – is something higher, something divine, a kind of "Unmoved Mover", a metaphysical origin of all physically existent things, be they plants, animals or human beings.

Because the sun, as Plato repeatedly stresses in his analogy, gives life. It causes flowers, meadows and fields to develop, grow and flourish, yet is itself subject to no change or alteration. That is to say, the sun is the sole thing not subjected to the law of coming to be and passing away. It is, indeed, the cause of these latter processes; but, as to itself, it has always been what it is and always will be. All this also applies, Plato argues, to the Idea of the Good. This Idea enables human beings to know the truth but is not itself identical with the truth; rather, it is truth's cause:

> Then what gives the truth to what is known and the ability to know to the knower, you must say, is the Idea of the Good. As it is the cause of knowledge and truth, consider it an object of knowledge. But beautiful as are both of these, knowledge and truth, if you think the Good to be something even more beautiful than these, you will think about it in the right way. [38]

Knowledge and truth, then, are themselves good and "commune with" the Idea of the Good. But they are not identical with the Good itself.

This construction of Plato's – whereby knowledge of beings which come to be and pass away refers us to something "higher" which does not itself belong to the order of beings – was the beginning of Western metaphysics, which taught that all that is physically existent can only be understood by reference to something "metaphysical" (i.e. something that lies beyond the physical realm). For Plato, the soul or mind can, indeed, "commune with" the Idea of the Good but this Idea has its origin in a source outside the soul or mind. It was just this difference – the difference between, on the one hand, the being of merely existent physical entities and, on the other, our capacity to know these entities only with the aid of something which pointed out beyond their sphere of mere being – that philosophers later came to call the "ontological difference".

We are now in the very heart of Plato's philosophy. Since our soul can "commune with" the eternal Ideas, a path to truth and to light opens up for us. Because every human being is endowed with the capacity to open his soul to the Idea of the Good and to recognize truth. But in everyday life we often let ourselves be distracted from this ideal and get lured away by projections and illusions. Plato's most famous description of this is his analogy of the cave (sometimes called "the allegory of the cave").

The Analogy of the Cave

In order to know the Good, Man must leave the world of everyday opinions and prejudices behind him and ascend, step by step, to the truth and to the light. Plato describes this freeing of the soul from the everyday world of illusions through the analogy of an arduous climb out of a dark subterranean cave. In *The Republic*, Plato's Socrates exhorts his interlocutors to imagine the bleak situation of men who spend their whole lives in such a cave:

> Imagine people, as it were, in an underground dwelling like a cave with a long wide entrance facing the light along the whole length of the cave. They have been

> there since childhood, shackled by the legs and the neck, so that they remain in the same spot, facing only forward, unable to turn their heads right around because of the chains. [39]

A group of men, then, are sitting with their backs to the cave entrance. Since their bonds prevent them from turning around, they stare, all their lives, at the cave wall facing them. Behind their backs runs a kind of road along which men carry various objects. This road is illuminated by a burning fire, so that the vague shadows of the objects and the men carrying them are thrown by the blazing flames onto the cave wall. Since the men facing the wall have been shackled in this position all their lives and have never seen anything else, they take these projected shadows of men and objects not for shadows but for real things. They even give these shadow figures names and talk about them as if they really existed. How, since they can never turn around toward the light, could they ever realize that these things are actually mere optical illusions?

> And what if the prison chamber were to throw back echoes from the wall in front whenever any of the passers-by spoke; do you think they would think this was anything but the passing shadows speaking? [40]

But now it becomes really interesting. Plato next has Socrates propose the following scenario:

> Whenever anyone was freed and suddenly made to stand up, look around, walk, and look up toward the light [...] what do you think he would say [...]? [41]

Such a man would have no choice but to gradually recognize that the shadows on the wall were not real and that he had been the dupe, all his life up to this point, of mere artificial projections. A painful insight. And if he were to continue to climb upward, he would come directly to perceive not just the road with people passing and the light of the fire but, in the end, even the daylight that shines through the cave entrance. Blinded by this light, he would first gaze out over the sea in which the clouds and the landscape around the cave are reflected. These reflections, too, he would at first take for realities. But finally he would succeed in directing his gaze upon the real landscape and the real sky. Finally, at the end of his ascent, he might even be able to turn his gaze toward the sun itself, the true force of light which gives to all other things their visibility and their reality. This first sight of the sun, Plato's Socrates contends, would necessarily be something overwhelming for such a man:

> Then finally he would be able to see the sun, I think [...] And straight after this he would be able to infer about it that this is what

Plato's Central Idea

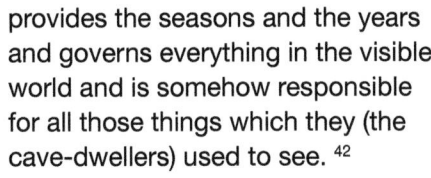

provides the seasons and the years and governs everything in the visible world and is somehow responsible for all those things which they (the cave-dwellers) used to see. [42]

With this analogy Plato wants to make clear to us that, in his daily life, Man is surrounded by many phantasms and illusions and has lost all sight of the truth. Just like the men fettered in the cave, we often consider things to be important which are not so at all. We allow our minds to be impressed by mere shadows, instead of freeing ourselves, climbing upward, and opening ourselves to the world of the Ideas. We do not do this because we tend to love comfort and be afraid of change.

Climbing out of the cave is an arduous task, which is why most people are content to continue taking mere shadows for realities. This is also the reason why people tend to show no gratitude but rather, on the contrary, show irritation when someone who has seen the sun – that is to say, the Idea of the Good, the True and the Beautiful – descends back into the cave and informs them that their poor world consists only of illusions.

Were such a one to do even more than this and attempt to free his shackled comrades and persuade them to make the ascent into the light as well he would most likely, Plato's Socrates speculates, provoke much worse than just irritation. The cave-dwellers would actually try to take his life:

> [...] Would he not set the others laughing and would it not be said of him that, in going up to the top, he had come back with his eyesight ruined, and that it wasn't worth even attempting to go up there? And if they could somehow get their hands on him and kill him, wouldn't they put the man to death who had tried to free them and lead them upward? [43]

This passage in the famous cave analogy surely alludes to the fate which Plato, who was writing this many years after his teacher's death, knew Socrates himself to have suffered. Because Socrates, who had all his life tried to lead his fellow Athenians toward the light and had insistently called for them to live more morally, was eventually condemned to death by them as an agitator.

Still today, the analogy of the cave stands as an exhortation to us not to rest complacently content with the manipulated world of direct sense-perception. Because, Plato tells us, every one of us has the chance to shake off his fetters and ascend to the truth.

The Ideal State

Because, however, but a few of us are really able to follow the light of truth to the highest levels, it is these few alone who should be entrusted with the governance of the state.

This is why, Plato argued, no one could be better guaranteed to govern a state well than a class of true philosophers:

> Unless philosophers become kings in our states [...] or those we now call kings and potentates genuinely and competently pursue philosophy [...] there can be no respite from evil in the state [...] nor, in my view, even in the human race. [44]

Only philosophers can handle matters of state in a way that will be just and free of corruption. The ideal form of the state is then, for Plato, aristocracy in the literal sense of the Greek word: "rule by the best". This may seem surprising, since already in Plato's era there existed the first democratically-organized city-states. But Plato clearly preferred aristocracy over democracy. He had a deep mistrust of rule by the people. His masterpiece, *The Republic*, contains a powerful warning against the negative consequences of democracy. Giving voting rights to all citizens would be very dangerous, he warned, because the common people might be all too easily impressed and manipulated by a bright and loud campaign:

Plato's Central Idea

> I imagine that those who love listening and watching eagerly pursue beautiful sounds and colours and shapes and everything made up of such things. But their minds are incapable of seeing and pursuing the nature of Beauty itself. [...] Then we won't be too far out if we refer to them as 'belief-lovers' rather than lovers of wisdom? [45]

It is because the mass of the people falls so easily for mere opinions and prejudices that there is always a danger that it will elect whomever presents himself in the brightest colours and speaks with the loudest voice. Thus democracy constantly threatens to slip into tyranny:

> And doesn't this mean that the people habitually appoint someone outstanding to take charge of them, nurturing him and making him great? [46]

Such a popular leader, lauded by the common people, tends, Plato argues, to become drunk with his newly-gained power. Using the police and judges dependent on him, he establishes a reign of terror and misuses the law. He arrests, and convicts on groundless charges, any citizens who displease him, or exiles, deports or even murders them, like a wild beast that has tasted blood:

So isn't it the same with the man who leads the people who, having taken over a really docile crowd, does not withhold his hand from shedding the blood of his fellow tribesmen, but unjustly brings charges of murder to the law-courts, as indeed usually happens, thereby wiping out a man's life, tasting kindred blood with impious tongue and mouth, and exiles and executes […]? [47]

It need not even be pointed out that the first thing that such a brutal demagogue will do after his election is abolish the right to vote and declare himself ruler for life. For Plato, then, the basic problem of democracy is that free voters belonging to a free people can at any time choose to replace this freedom with the worst kind of slavery by electing a tyrannical demagogue:

> It seems that excessive freedom both in our private lives and public evolves into nothing other than excessive slavery [...]. So it's likely, then, that tyranny is based on no other political system than democracy; out of the highest freedom [...] comes the most widespread and savage slavery. [48]

Such slavery, Plato has Socrates go on, can often only be removed by the tyrant's defeat in conflict with foreign enemies. Plato foresees here, over two thousand years before the fact but in terrifyingly concrete detail, the fate suffered by a country like Germany in the 20th Century. Today, almost all modern democracies have introduced clauses into their constitutions which make such a self-abolition of democracy impossible. But Plato's concern here remains a comprehensible one. Consequently, then, also his solution. To exclude the possibility that dangerous men, or even simply mediocre ones, should come to power through election, Plato proposes a system different from democracy. In the future state which he envisages those who hold public office are to be selected solely on the basis of whether they are able to bring to realization the highest Idea of the Good and of Justice:

> [...] This is how these things appear to me: in the knowable region the Idea of the Good is the last among the things perceived and is seen with difficulty; but, once seen, then it is to be reckoned as the origin of all that is right and good for everyone [...]. And he who is going to act with good sense in private or public life must see this (Idea of the Good). [49]

If a state has governors at its head who have truly gained a view of the Idea of the Good, these governors will rule the people with the greatest possible wisdom and love. These governors, then, must be true philosophers. But how are such "philosopher-kings" to be found? Who shall seek them out?

Plato takes his bearings here from the nature of the soul. Just as the soul, in the "analogy of the chariot" which we examined above, consisted of the three regions Eros, self-assertion and Reason, so is Plato's ideal state to consist of a farmer, guardian and philosopher caste. Plato envisages farmers and craftsmen devoting themselves, by their very nature, to feeding the state, making it prosperous and ensuring the race's continuation, just as the armed guardians devote themselves, by their nature, to defending the state and asserting its interests, and the philosopher-kings, by theirs, to its rational and just governance.

In accordance with the model of the soul, the farmers and craftsmen are permitted to indulge desire and may, therefore, possess money and property of all kinds. The guardians, by contrast, are distinguished by strength of will and disciplined self-assertion, being prepared for this function by physical training and the strictest education. The third and highest caste, the philosopher-kings, devote themselves exclusively to the service of the state and form its government. This caste stands for the rational part of the soul; it is the "charioteer" who guides the willpower and the desire of the two lower castes, with wisdom, in the right direction.

Although this ideal state envisaged by Plato is hierarchically divided into three castes – one might say, three classes – there exists the possibility of social mobility. In Plato's ideal state everyone has an equal chance to become a philosopher-king. All the children are given equal educational opportunity, regardless of the origin or income of their parents. Only after an intensive shared education in gymnastics, music, mathematics and dialectic is there organized, for twenty-year-old citizens, a strict and impartial examination which establishes the best and sets these off from the others. After another ten years a second examination is held and those who pass this begin a special schooling in philosophy. They are also schooled in music, art and literature (although, surprisingly, Plato views Hesiod and parts of Homer as unsuitable for inclusion here, since they tend to weaken the will). Finally, from the age of thirty-five on, these citizens must once again prove their practical skill and spend fifteen years gaining real experience of war among the guardian class. Only then

Plato's Central Idea

are those who have proven themselves the best here too appointed to governmental positions as philosopher-kings.

Gender plays no role here. Both men and women can be appointed as guardians and philosopher-rulers to protect the state. Women's lesser physical strength, Plato believed, could be compensated by skill and other virtues:

> Then a woman will have the same nature in respect of becoming a guardian of our state as a male [...]. [50]

Whether man or woman, the decisive thing is that every citizen of the state is selected and deployed according to his or her merits and capacities. Plato thinks that assigning individuals to three castes makes good sense because it means that each person will be able to contribute to the state's welfare in the way that suits him or her best:

For Plato, then, justice does not consist in all citizens earning the same amount of money or doing the same thing but rather in each one "having and doing his (or her) own". Plato's ideal state demands much more selfless commitment and self-sacrifice, for example, from its leading functionaries, the guardians and philosophers, than it does from the third caste – much more, indeed, even than is demanded from today's politicians and economic elites. It is a basic rule that neither guardians nor philosopher-kings can own any material property, so that they cannot even be tempted to use their positions of power to their own advantage. They are even prescribed especially modest diets and habitations:

Plato's Central Idea

> First of all, none of them is to have acquired any personal property which is not absolutely necessary. Then, none must have any dwelling or storehouse of any sort to which there is not free access to anyone who wishes to enter. They will have such supplies as men need who are [...]

> sound of mind, and courageous, covenanting from the rest of the citizens to receive so much pay for their duties as guardians that they will not have a surplus nor a shortfall at the end of the year. They will eat regularly in a mess and live together like troops in a camp [...]. [52]

The guardians and philosopher-kings, then, live in a kind of commune in which sexual liberty reigns between men and women. Marriage with a single spouse is forbidden to them, as is private family life with children of their own, so as to preclude fathers or mothers using their state positions to secure advantages for their offspring. Plato is ruthlessly consistent in thinking out this concept, designing his state to neutralize even such powerful basic feelings as parental love:

> These women shall all be the common property of all the men; no one of them shall live with any man privately. Their children too shall be held in common and no parent shall know his or her offspring nor any child his or her parent. [53]

The children are cared for first by nurses and then collectively, in huge children's homes, by all the male and female guardians together, so that each receives equal love from each. Since no one knows whether they are dealing, in any case, with their own child or someone else's, each child is handled with great care. Plato even recommends, with a view to maintaining a stable population and "the quality of the flock", a governmental control of sexual intercourse aimed at favouring "the best men and the best women". The philosopher-kings are to organize festivals and mass marriages in order to spur on, or discourage, procreation:

Plato's Central Idea

> From what we have agreed [...] our best men should make their match with the best women as often as possible; but with men and women of lower status, it's the reverse. We must nurture the offspring of the first group but not those of the second, if our flock is to be of the highest quality. And all such goings-on must be kept hidden from all but the rulers themselves, if indeed our 'herd' of guardians is to be free, as far as possible, from internal factions. [54]

To us today, these eugenic measures sound even more sinister and disturbing than Plato's forbidding the guardians and the philosopher-kings to have belongings, households and families of their own. But what Plato was really aiming at with these radical measures was the unification of wisdom and power. He wanted to ensure at any price that the guardians and philosopher-kings remained, all their lives, incorruptible and devoted themselves solely to the general good. Having neither family nor house nor money of their own, they would place all their powers in the service of the people and of the realization of the Idea of the Good.

In a work of his last years, *The Laws*, Plato takes back a number of the radical demands he had raised in *The Republic*. This later work is not so much a theoretical call for an ideal state as a series of pragmatic suggestions for the improvement of really existing ones. To this end, he no longer emphasizes so much the role of philosopher-kings, concentrating rather on the need for good laws and good institutions.

Of What Use is Plato's Discovery for Us Today?

The Ideal State – Vision or Nightmare?

It must be admitted from the start that Plato's vision of an ideal state seems, from our present-day perspective, unattractive, even repulsive. Who, today, would wish to live in a caste society in which free individual self-development is so rigorously restricted? The leading classes in Plato's ideal state, the guardians and the philosophers, must accept separation from their own children and get by without any kind of private sphere. They must also undergo, almost their whole life long, rigorous selection examinations. The lower caste of farmers and craftsmen leads a less restricted existence but just because of this it is completely without a political voice. Its members have no right to vote and are completely excluded from affairs of state.

But it is above all the eugenicist measures proposed by Plato with a view to optimising the genetic stock of the guardian class which awaken, after the recent historical experiences of racism and Nazism, our deep mistrust and make Plato's utopia appear (at least at first sight) from our present viewpoint rather as a nightmare.

For this reason, Plato's concept of a mental and spiritual aristocracy has been massively criticized from various sides. The philosopher Karl Popper, for example, even counted Plato among the intellectual forebears of totalitarianism. In his book *The Open Society and Its Enemies* Popper accuses Plato of having, with his doctrine of the Ideas and his concept of an ideal state, claimed a totalitarian right of governance. Plato justifies, Popper claims, the absolute power of the philosopher-kings with the notion of their privileged access to the Idea of the Good; since the philosopher-kings alone, due to their training and talent, are able to know the Idea of the Good, and thus the truth, it is they who have the natural right and the duty to govern all other citizens and to see to their welfare. For Popper, however, such a claim to being the sole possessor(s) of truth and thus requiring no democratic legitimation for one's governance constitutes arrogance, ideology and false consciousness.

The philosopher Bertrand Russell, in concurral with Popper's charge of totalitarianism, tried to show that not just the clerical class which provided the dignitaries and functionaries of the Christian church in the Middle Ages but also the National Socialist and Communist parties of the modern age stood very much in the totalitarian tradition of Plato as regards their legitimations of their rule.

The powerful dignitaries of the Catholic clergy, for example, drew their authority, just like Plato's philosopher-kings, solely from their supposed nearness to God, to Whom they devoted their lives, as well as from their years of training in Bible study and the Latin language. Like the guardians and philosophers of Plato's Republic, these mighty clerics possessed a monopoly on education and lived, familyless, in closed communities. And also like Plato's guardians, Popper points out, this clerical caste had attained their high and powerful positions without being elected by the people. Dictatorial party elites too, he goes on, who have evoked principles like "the Party is always right" or Marxist, racist or nationalist truths, stand directly in the descendancy of Plato's thought. Such elites, Popper suggests, have legitimated their rule just as Plato's philosophers do: by claiming to possess a higher form of thought and a more direct access to the truth.

But for Popper the essence of the open society is that every one of its members can contribute to it a truth of his own. This means that each member too, be he simple citizen or leading politician, must concede that he may have erred and that the truth he believes he possesses might have to be corrected. Nor must one ever treat even scientific truths as absolutes, argues Popper. As soon as a theory is falsified – i.e. if a counter-example to it, or an error in it, is discovered – it must be revised or replaced by a more correct one. Because every theory is necessarily flawed. This fallibility of all knowledge must be acknowledged, insists Popper. Plato, however, he goes on, had sketched out, with his conception of infallible philosopher-kings, a totalitarian state which was without basis because without room for criticism.

It is interesting that Popper cites in support of his demand for falsifiability none other than Socrates as this latter was portrayed by Plato in *The Apology*, one of the earliest Platonic dialogues. The portrait given in such early texts, contends Popper, matches the real historical Socrates who (so Popper claims) had been a "falsificationist" like himself – i.e. he had self-critically accepted his own limits and recognized that there can be no eternally binding single truth.

If one holds to this originally Socratic notion, then politics can only be practiced according to the principle of trial and error and never with any such claim to absolute knowledge as is raised by the philosopher-kings. Plato, claims Popper, had faithfully portrayed, in *The Apology*, the stance of the real Socrates but had later abandoned this fidelity and replaced Socrates's stance with his own doctrine of the Ideas and striving for absolute Good.

But recent scholarship has cast doubt on whether there really is such a radical break between the Socrates portrayed in Plato's early dialogues and the Socrates who propounds the doctrine of the Ideas. The Socrates whom Plato shows us in the early dialogues has not yet, indeed, called for an ascent of the mind to the Idea of the Good and to the Divine, but all that he says certainly presupposes that an absolute truth exists. It is only on the basis of such a presupposition that he can critique all the views of the Sophists as errors. Nor was Socrates's starting point, as Popper claims, an absolute not-knowing but rather the application of the dialectical question-and-answer method with the aim of pushing to the heart of a problem and thereby to the truth itself.

The charge of totalitarianism is also questionable, for several reasons. Firstly, Plato's model of an ideal state was always aimed at the goal of ensuring justice for all citizens. Plato does not plan, in his ideal state, for that subordination or manipulation, through "mass organizations", of all institutions and civil groups which is typical of totalitarian polities. The large caste of farmers and manual workers is free to develop whatever private, family or economic structures it desires to.

The rules and examinations applying to the guardian and philosopher castes likewise – authoritarian though they are – only serve the aim of producing, instead of tyrants, ideal statesmen and -women for high governmental positions. Thanks to their strict moral education and their renunciation of private property they should, by rights, always place the public interest over their own.

Thirdly, given their long philosophical education, Plato's philosopher-kings remain always morally committed to the Ideas of the Good and of Justice, so that rule by terror and genocide are courses excluded in principle for them. Even if it remains, in Plato's dialogues, insufficiently concrete for it to be really rationally analysed, it is clear that the "Good in itself" which is alluded to in the famous "analogies" is something incompatible with nationalist, racist, chauvinist or other goals of an ideological nature. It was, after all, Plato himself who repeatedly criticized tyranny and oligarchy as forms of despotism.

But above all it must be borne in mind, when judging Plato's ideal state, that *The Republic* was written two and a half thousand years ago, so that it would indeed be a miracle if Plato's political concept matched, in all respects, our understanding of democracy. We must see Plato's historical achievement to lie rather in the fact that he was the first man to develop any sort of theoretical model of the state and thus place at humanity's disposal a conceptual resource which made it possible to critically analyze and oppose those real states and governments with which citizens found themselves faced. Plato was the first thinker to cease to look on rulership in the way it had been looked on for thousands of years – as something natural and unquestionable – and to view it rather as something created by Man that needs to be justified.

Plato justifies the legitimacy of the rule of the philosopher-kings by reference to their many years of physical and moral training and to their performances in examinations. He does not, indeed, at all try to justify his state in terms of political freedom and the self-determination of all citizens. But nonetheless, *The Republic* represents the introduction into human culture, once and for all, of the notion that rulership has a duty to provide a justification for its existence.

Plato knew very well what historical force could be

derived from such a theoretical model, even if he was aware that the specific state proposed by him would never be historically realized:

Whether in Thomas More's *Utopia*, in the different "social contract" theories of Hobbes and Rousseau or, closer to our own time, in the "choice made behind a veil of ignorance" envisaged in John Rawls's *Theory of Justice*, philosophers have followed Plato in speculating as to what an ideal, perfectly just state would look like and thereby, at the same time, criticizing existing states. Even if, in the course of two and a half thousand years, the answers given have changed and today the rule of the people has tended to take the place of the rule of philosopher-kings, Plato remains nonetheless the forefather of the key notion that state power is always under an obligation to justify itself.

Plato – The Thinker Who Laid the Foundations of the West

But it is not only political science that takes its origins from Plato. Plato's thought also prefigures Christianity and he can thus be said to have left his mark on the entire history of the West. Plato remains, even today, the most frequently-cited philosopher in the world. The British philosopher and mathematician Alfred North Whithead even went so far as to write that the whole of Western philosophy is essentially just a series of "footnotes to Plato". [56]

The Christian religion did indeed draw heavily upon Plato's ideas and he has remained down the centuries a source of inspiration for Christian thought. This applies not only to the doctrine of the Ideas but also to the figure of Socrates. Just a glance at the fate suffered by the latter reveals many important points in common with the fate suffered by Jesus: both believed in the immortality of the soul; both were tried and condemned to death by secular state institutions; both refused to flee when they could and chose rather to die for their convictions; both, with their honest and consistent stances, gave unmistakable testimony to the truth that earthly life is less important than remaining always open to the Divine.

Socrates's belief in the immortality of the soul, and in that Good in Itself which underlies all earthly life and alone gives meaning and purpose to this latter, became part of the foundation of Christianity. For Socrates as for Jesus everything that is material, however beautiful or charming, is of no more than fleeting value. What matters in the end in life is opening one's soul to the eternal and the divine. For Plato as for Christianity, life on earth is only a kind of test of our character. We prove ourselves by turning our soul toward the Good and keeping ourselves free from material passions like envy, hatred, resentment, vanity and greed. Both Socrates and Jesus were decided opponents of materialism; they were concerned above all with inner values. We see this in the little prayer offered up by Socrates toward the end of the *Phaedrus*:

Of What Use ist Plato's Discovery for Us Today?

> O beloved Pan and all ye other gods of this place, grant to me that I be made beautiful in my soul within, and that all external possessions be in harmony with my inner man. [57]

Plato himself, although the son of a rich and noble Athenian family, led a very modest life. He instructed the students in the school he founded, the Academy, free of charge. Plato's life and his philosophy are, still today, a call to live a temperate life.

But even if Plato prepared the way for Christianity, there are of course also great differences between his ideas and the latter. Christians view Jesus as the Son of God and as God's incarnation on earth, believing that he even worked miracles. But Socrates was only a philosopher. He turned his mind and soul, indeed, toward the divine and the eternal Ideas. But he always remained just a human being. What concerned him was knowledge, not faith.

Another difference from Christianity is that in Plato

"radical Evil" plays no role. Man can, by being a wise man or a fool, either pursue, or neglect to pursue, the building of his soul to higher things; but Man is not suspended here, as later in Christianity, between Good and Evil in the sense of God and the Devil. We find in Plato no such autonomous pole of pure evil as Christianity's Satan, Mephisto or Lucifer; everything is illuminated by the light of the Good, even if we do not always recognize it. This is why, instead of guilt or sin, we find in Plato rather merely a "closed-mindedness", a lack of formation and cultivation which can be remedied, through reincarnation, in another life. Once Christianity emerged, Plato's followers, the Platonists, were careful to set the doctrine of the Ideas clearly off from Christian teachings.

Plato was through and through an idealist. The few attempts he made to intervene in material life and change some aspects of reality were failures on a massive scale. On one occasion he accepted an invitation from Dionysius the Elder, tyrant of Syracuse, to become his political counsellor and put his ideas about the ideal state into practice in that city. His student and friend Dion had introduced him to Dionysius and given him this precious opportunity. But it was not long before Plato and the stubborn tyrant fell out. He fell from favour at Dionysius's court and, if stories circulated at the time are to be credited, was even sold by the tyrant into slavery. Fortunately, a friend bought his freedom and he was able to return to Athens unharmed. If we ask, then, what use Plato's work can be to us today, then we must answer that this use does not consist in his actual political deeds, nor even in his model of an ideal state, but rather in his tireless encouragement to develop the mind and soul to higher levels.

We Are All Prisoners – the Ascent to the Good, the True and the Beautiful

Whoever opens their mind and soul to the Ideas of the Good, the True and the Beautiful, says Plato, will achieve complete harmony and inner contentment. But this is not so easy. Plato stresses again and again that, in order to gain such a harmony of soul, we need to be constantly working on ourselves. Formulated in modern terms, he tells us we must be ready for "lifelong learning". By this he means, of course, not professional qualification but the forming of our learning capacity and the willingness to be truthful. We have to learn to see with the inner eye. Only when, as in the analogy of the cave, we open ourselves to the light of the sun and of knowledge of the Good are we able to ascend toward the truth. But what does this mean concretely?

Plato would advise us to withdraw, at least from time to time, from hectic modern life and ask ourselves some essential questions: are we still standing upon the ground of truth or is our life, in certain areas, an untruthful one? And if so – why? Are our relationships real or have they already been dulled by deceit, apathy or loss of trust? Are we being submerged in our daily duties and in the charms of capitalist consumerism, or can we succeed in turning our gaze toward the essential? Are we already Internet and TV junkies who, instead of the real world, are trapped in media projections and illusions? Or, to adopt Plato's provocative image: are we still free, or do we live the lives of "plovers", losing ourselves in brief enjoyments?

These thoughts all culminate in the simple question: is our life a good one? There is probably no one who could reply with an unconditional "yes" to this question. And yet it makes sense to ask it. It is important to allow the truth to emerge even if, as Plato constantly stresses, it can be painful to do so. Just as the shackled man in the analogy of the cave frees himself only with difficulty from his fetters, slowly ascends, and is dazzled by the ever stronger light, so too is it hard to admit to oneself that one has fallen victim, be it for a long or just a short while, to an illusion and that one must now leave the world one is familiar with. Every profound change makes one afraid, whether it be a change of job, separation from a life-partner, or the forming of a completely new life-plan that dispenses with material security.

But Plato encourages us to open our souls to the truth nonetheless and to focus our gaze on the essential. Because one thing is certain: in a certain sense we are all prisoners, bedazzled by a world of mere appearances. For example, if one lives in an inauthentic world, or in a relationship where feelings are not openly addressed, much that was once beautiful can become ugly. Tempting as it is to cover over inconsistencies in our lives or to rationalize and thereby justify them, one's inner feelings – or, as Plato says, one's soul – cannot be fooled. Conversely, one's feelings become in many respects clearer and more beautiful if one lives as one's heart prompts one. A fulfilled life is only possible if one acts with honesty and authenticity:

> Then it seems that virtue would be a kind of health, beauty and good condition of the soul, while evil is sickness, a disgrace and a weakness. [58]

The soul feels a lifelong need for harmony. But harmony only arises when one turns one's attention to the Good, the True and the Beautiful. If we bear this in mind, we see that Plato's analogy of the cave remains as relevant today as it was when it was written.

If we are to make fruitful the notion Plato expresses with his analogies of the cave and the sun, we must go forth and seek the path of ascent – ascent to the light and to the Good. But at this point we are obliged to answer one last, and decisive, question: what exactly is "the Good"?

Ultimate Knowledge as a Spur and Source of Strength

Plato is concerned with more than just the individual's freeing himself from self-forgetfulness and imprisonment in worlds of mere appearance. In their search for happiness and harmony of soul, human beings must take a last step beyond just authenticity vis-à-vis themselves and others – into a final comprehensive knowledge. The mind must be opened for a "communing" with the highest Idea of all, the Idea of the Good. To behold this Idea of the Good in all its beauty and distinctness is, for Plato, nothing else than to come to feel that divine energy which alone endows with meaning all that we encounter in the world. It is for this reason that Plato exhorts us, in his late work *The Laws*, to make the Divine the measure of all our aspirations and actions:

Plato contradicts here not only the Sophists' claim that "Man is the measure of all things" but also the widespread modern notion of personal self-realization. For Plato, the Idea of the Good is the true and original divine power, in whose light everything shines and which alone gives us certainty regarding what is just, true and beautiful.

There is no doubt that Plato's philosophy has a strong spiritual core. He repeatedly draws mythological and religious motifs, such as the transmigration of souls, into his thought. Perhaps this is why what Plato has to say about immortality and the quest for the Good has remained alive from antiquity, through the Christian Middle Ages, up to post-modern spiritual worldviews. But the inmost core of his teachings has always retained a certain mystery.

The notion which shines out over everything he wrote – the Idea of the Good, or what Plato calls "the Divine" – was described by him only through analogies and was not really deciphered in any of his dialogues. Because, Plato states, it would have been impossible to do so.

Words and language simply fail one when one tries to make the Divine and the Good in itself into objects of knowledge:

Of What Use ist Plato´s Discovery for Us Today?

There does not exist, nor will there ever exist, any treatise of mine dealing therewith. For it does not at all admit of verbal expression like other studies but (only) as a result of continued application to the subject itself and communion therewith, it is brought to birth in the soul on a sudden, as light that is kindled by a leaping spark, and thereafter it nourishes itself. [60]

Plato justifies, then, his silence about the nature of the Good with the fact that this latter cannot, like other items of knowledge, be summed up in a teachable doctrine without its substance thereby slipping away and becoming unfruitful:

> And if I had thought that these subjects ought to be fully stated in writing or in speech to the public, what nobler action could I have performed in my life than [...] bringing forth to the light for all men the nature of reality? But were I to undertake this task, it would not, as I think, prove a good thing for men [...]. [61]

Since Plato never defined the Good, we must rely on intuition and on our own spiritual experiences. Knowledge of the Good arises, as Plato says, finally only through "continued application" to this Good, through "communion therewith", so that "a light is brought to birth suddenly in the soul" which, once kindled, feeds and sustains its own self. Religiously and spiritually oriented people intuitively understand what Plato means when he encourages us to follow the path to the light and to make truth the food of our soul.

But Plato's legacy is enriching also for rationally thinking people. Because the inner connection between the Good, the True and the Beautiful can be grasped by all. Whatever is good and true always possesses an inner beauty, while whatever is false, injurious and malign appears ugly and repulsive. One need not, then, believe in the immortality of the soul in order to feel that, with the realization of the Ideas of the Good, the True and the Beautiful, Plato gave something tremendous to the world. His appeal to us is a constant thorn in the flesh of complacency and self-forgetfulness. Even if Plato nowhere provided the Ideas of the Good, the True and the Beautiful with verifiable criteria, so that these Ideas elude rational analysis, one senses nonetheless that there proceeds from the notion alone of these concepts an enormous force. What Plato prompts us to, across the many centuries, is to take part, with all our soul, in these concepts' unfolding:

Indeed, (the Good) is what every soul pursues and for the sake of which it does everything, [...] sensing instinctively that there is something great there. [62]

Bibliographical References:

Whenever possible, the passages cited are taken from the bilingual (Greek-English) editions of Plato's dialogues published by the Loeb Classical Library in association with Harvard University Press. One key revision has been made to the Loeb translations – which are the work of different scholars, depending upon the dialogue – throughout: the translation of Plato's Greek term idea – which appears in some of the Loeb texts as 'Form' – is altered here, uniformly, to 'Idea'.

1. Plato, The Republic, Books 1-5, Loeb Classical Library Volume 237 (Harvard University Press, Cambridge Massachussetts, 2013) pp. 539-541 (Stephanus 473 d-e)
2. Plato, The Apology of Socrates, in Loeb Classical Library Volume 36 (Harvard University Press, Cambridge Massachusetts, 1990), p. 83 (Stephanus 21d)
3. Plato, The Republic, Books 6-10, Loeb Classical Library Volume 276 (Harvard University Press, Cambridge Massachusetts, 2013) p. 175 (Stephanus 533d)
4. Ibid. p. 93 (Stephanus 508e)
5. Ibid. p. 79 (Stephanus 505a)
6. Plato, Gorgias in Loeb Classical Library Volume 166 (Harvard University Press, Cambridge Massachusetts, 1991), p. 341 (Stephanus 470e)
7. Plato, The Republic, Books 6-10, Loeb Classical Library Volume 276 (Harvard University Press, Cambridge Massachusetts, 2013) p. 111 (Stephanus 515d)
8. Plato, Phaedrus, in Loeb Classical Library Volume 36 (Harvard University Press, Cambridge Massachusetts, 1990) p. 473 (Stephanus 246b)
9. Plato, Phaedo, in Loeb Classical Library Volume 36 (Harvard University Press, Cambridge Massachusetts, 1990) p. 225 (Stephanus 64d)
10. Ibid. (Stephanus 64e)

11 Plato, Phaedrus, in Loeb Classical Library Volume 36 (Harvard University Press, Cambridge Massachusetts, 1990) pp. 501-503 (Stephanus 256b)
12 Plato, Symposium in Loeb Classical Library Volume 166 (Harvard University Press, Cambridge Massachusetts, 1991) p. 101 (Stephanus 178c)
13 Ibid. pp. 101-103 (Stephanus 178e)
14 Ibid. p. 199 (Stephanus 208e)
15 Ibid. (Stephanus 209b)
16 Ibid. (Stephanus 210e) (translation slightly revised)
17 Ibid. (Stephanus 211c-d)
18 Plato, The Republic, Books 6-10, Loeb Classical Library Volume 276 (Harvard University Press, Cambridge Massachusetts, 2013) p. 79 (Stephanus 505b)
19 Plato, Gorgias in Loeb Classical Library Volume 166 (Harvard University Press, Cambridge Massachusetts, 1991), p. 419 (Stephanus 494b)
20 Plato, Symposium in Loeb Classical Library Volume 166 (Harvard University Press, Cambridge Massachusetts, 1991) p. 187 (Stephanus 205d)
21 Plato, The Republic, Books 6-10, Loeb Classical Library Volume 276 (Harvard University Press, Cambridge Massachusetts, 2013) p. 101 (Stephanus 510e) (translation slightly revised)
22 Plato, Symposium in Loeb Classical Library Volume 166 (Harvard University Press, Cambridge Massachusetts, 1991) p. 205 (Stephanus 211b)
23 Plato, Phaedo, in Loeb Classical Library Volume 36 (Harvard University Press, Cambridge Massachusetts, 1990) p. 345 (Stephanus 100d)
24 Ibid. p. 263 (Stephanus 75d)
25 Plato, Meno in Loeb Classical Library Volume 165 (Harvard University Press, Cambridge Massachusetts, 1990) p. 321 (Stephanus 86a)
26 Ibid. p. 303 (Stephanus 81 c-d)
27 Plato, Phaedo, in Loeb Classical Library Volume 36 (Harvard University Press, Cambridge Massachusetts, 1990) p. 283 (Stephanus 81b)
28 Ibid. p. 285 (Stephanus 81e)

29 Ibid. (Stephanus 81e-82a)
30 Ibid. p. 221 (Stephanus 63c)
31 Ibid. p. 223 (Stephanus 64a)
32 Ibid. p. 289 (Stephanus 82e)
33 Plato, Gorgias in Loeb Classical Library Volume 166 (Harvard University Press, Cambridge Massachusetts, 1991), p. 415 (Stephanus 493a)
34 Plato, Phaedrus, in Loeb Classical Library Volume 36 (Harvard University Press, Cambridge Massachusetts, 1990) pp. 469-471 (Stephanus 245d-e and 246a)
35 Plato, The Republic, Books 6-10, Loeb Classical Library Volume 276 (Harvard University Press, Cambridge Massachusetts, 2013) p. 91 (Stephanus 508d)
36 Ibid. pp. 91-93 (Stephanus 508d)
37 Ibid. pp. 93-95 (Stephanus 509b)
38 Ibid. p. 93 (Stephanus 508e)
39 Ibid. p. 107 (Stephanus 514a and b)
40 Ibid. p. 109 (Stephanus 515 b)
41 Ibid. pp. 109-111 (Stephanus 515c and d)
42 Ibid. p. 113 (Stephanus 516b and c)
43 Ibid. p. 115 (Stephanus 516e and 517a)
44 Plato, The Republic, Books 1-5, Loeb Classical Library Volume 237 (Harvard University Press, Cambridge Massachusetts, 2013) pp. 539-541 (Stephanus 473 d-e)
45 Ibid. pp. 549 and 567 (Stephanus 476b, 480a)
46 Plato, The Republic, Books 6-10, Loeb Classical Library Volume 276 (Harvard University Press, Cambridge Massachusetts, 2013) p. 289 (Stephanus 565c)
47 Ibid. p. 291 (Stephanus 565e and 566a)
48 Ibid. p. 283 (Stephanus 564a)
49 Ibid. p. 117 (Stephanus 517b and c)
50 Plato, The Republic, Books 1-5, Loeb Classical Library Volume 237 (Harvard University Press, Cambridge Massachusetts, 2013) p. 471 (Stephanus 456a)
51 Ibid. p. 397 (Stephanus 434a)
52 Ibid. p. 337 (Stephanus 416d and e)
53 Ibid. pp. 477-79 (Stephanus 457d)
54 Ibid. p. 487 (Stephanus 459e)

55 Plato, The Republic, Books 6-10, Loeb Classical Library Volume 276 (Harvard University Press, Cambridge Massachusetts, 2013) p. 389 (Stephanus 592b).
56 Alfred North Whitehead Process and Reality (Corrected Edition) The Free Press, New York, 1978, p. 39.
57 Plato, Phaedrus, in Loeb Classical Library Volume 36 (Harvard University Press, Cambridge Massachusetts, 1990) p. 579 (Stephanus 279b and c).
58 Plato, The Republic, Books 1-5, Loeb Classical Library Volume 237 (Harvard University Press, Cambridge Massachusetts, 2013) p. 439 (Stephanus 444d) (translation slightly revised).
59 Plato, The Laws, Books 1-6, Loeb Classical Library (Harvard University Press, Cambridge Massachusetts, 1984) p. 295 (Stephanus 716c).
60 Plato, Epistle VII, Loeb Classical Library Volume 234 (Harvard University Press, Cambridge Massachusetts, 1989) p. 531 (Stephanus 341c and d).
61 Plato, Epistle VII, Loeb Classical Library Volume 234 (Harvard University Press, Cambridge Massachusetts, 1989) pp. 531-533 (Stephanus 341d and e).
62 Plato, The Republic, Books 6-10, Loeb Classical Library Volume 276 (Harvard University Press, Cambridge Massachusetts, 2013) p. 81 (Stephanus 505e).

Already published in the same series:

Walther Ziegler
Camus in 60 Minutes
ISBN 9783741227738

Walther Ziegler
Freud in 60 Minutes
ISBN 9783741227707

Walther Ziegler
Hegel in 60 Minutes
ISBN 9783741227677

Walther Ziegler
Heidegger in 60 Minutes
ISBN 9783741227752

Walther Ziegler
Kant in 60 Minutes
ISBN 9783741226373

Walther Ziegler
Marx in 60 Minutes
ISBN 9783741227691

Walther Ziegler
Platon in 60 Minutes
ISBN 9783741227615

Walther Ziegler
Rousseau in 60 Minutes
ISBN 9783741227622

Walther Ziegler
Sartre in 60 Minutes
ISBN 9783741227653

Walther Ziegler
Smith in 60 Minutes
ISBN 9783741227721

Coming soon in the same series:

Walther Ziegler
Adorno in 60 Minutes

Walther Ziegler
Arendt in 60 Minutes

Walther Ziegler
Bacon in 60 Minutes

Walther Ziegler
Descartes in 60 Minutes

Walther Ziegler
Foucault in 60 Minutes

Walther Ziegler
Habermas in 60 Minutes

Walther Ziegler
Hobbes in 60 Minutes

Walther Ziegler
Nietzsche in 60 Minutes

Walther Ziegler
Popper in 60 Minutes

Walther Ziegler
Rawls in 60 Minutes

Walther Ziegler
Schopenhauer in 60 Minutes

Walther Ziegler
Wittgenstein in 60 Minutes

The author:

Dr Walther Ziegler is academically trained in the fields of philosophy, history and political science. As a foreign correspondent, reporter and newsroom coordinator for the German TV station ProSieben he has produced films on every continent. His news reports have won several prizes and awards. He has also authored numerous books in the field of philosophy. His many years of experience as a journalist mean that he is able to present the complex ideas of the great philosophers in a way that is both engaging and very clear. Since 2007 he has also been active as a teacher and trainer of young TV journalists in Munich, holding the post of Academic Director at the Media Academy, an institute of higher education that offers film and TV courses at its base directly on the site of the major European film production company Bavaria Film.